This book belongs to:

_____

_____

_____

INTERNET INFO & PERSONAL

Internet Service Provider:

Account Number:

Tech Support:

Customer Service:

Notes:

Email (personal)

Username:

Password:

Email (work)

Username:

Password:

Domain:

Mail Sever:

Notes:

SERVICE

Phone Provider 📞

USERNAME:

PASSWORD:

SECURITY QUESTION:

ANSWERS:

Cable Provider 📺

USERNAME:

PASSWORD:

SECURITY QUESTION :

ANSWERS:

Credit Card 💳

USERNAME:

PASSWORD:

SECURITY QUESTION:

ANSWERS:

SOCIAL MEDIA

Google

USERNAME:

PASSWORD:

SECURITY QUESTION:

ANSWERS:

YouTube

USERNAME:

PASSWORD:

SECURITY QUESTION:

ANSWERS:

Facebook

USERNAME:

PASSWORD:

SECURITY QUESTION:

ANSWERS:

SOCIAL MEDIA

Instagram

USERNAME:

PASSWORD:

SECURITY QUESTION :

ANSWERS:

Twitter

USERNAME:

PASSWORD:

SECURITY QUESTION:

ANSWERS:

Snapchat

USERNAME:

PASSWORD:

SECURITY QUESTION:

ANSWERS:

SOCIAL MEDIA & ETC

LinkedIn

USERNAME:

PASSWORD:

SECURITY QUESTION:

ANSWERS:

Yahoo

USERNAME:

PASSWORD:

SECURITY QUESTION:

ANSWERS:

Amazon

USERNAME:

PASSWORD:

SECURITY QUESTION:

ANSWERS:

A

WEBSITE:

USERNAME:

PASSWORD:

QUESTION:

ANSWER:

NOTES:

WEBSITE:

USERNAME:

PASSWORD:

QUESTION:

ANSWER:

NOTES:

WEBSITE:

USERNAME:

PASSWORD:

QUESTION:

ANSWER:

NOTES:

WEBSITE:

USERNAME:

PASSWORD:

QUESTION:

ANSWER:

NOTES:

WEBSITE:

USERNAME:

PASSWORD:

QUESTION:

ANSWER:

NOTES:

WEBSITE:

USERNAME:

PASSWORD:

QUESTION:

ANSWER:

NOTES:

A

WEBSITE:

USERNAME:

PASSWORD:

QUESTION:

ANSWER:

NOTES:

WEBSITE:

USERNAME:

PASSWORD:

QUESTION:

ANSWER:

NOTES:

WEBSITE:

USERNAME:

PASSWORD:

QUESTION:

ANSWER:

NOTES:

WEBSITE: _____

USERNAME: _____

PASSWORD: _____

QUESTION: _____

ANSWER: _____

NOTES: _____

_____

WEBSITE: _____

USERNAME: _____

PASSWORD: _____

QUESTION: _____

ANSWER: _____

NOTES: _____

_____

WEBSITE: _____

USERNAME: _____

PASSWORD: _____

QUESTION: _____

ANSWER: _____

NOTES: _____

_____

B

WEBSITE:

USERNAME:

PASSWORD:

QUESTION:

ANSWER:

NOTES:

WEBSITE:

USERNAME:

PASSWORD:

QUESTION:

ANSWER:

NOTES:

WEBSITE:

USERNAME:

PASSWORD:

QUESTION:

ANSWER:

NOTES:

B

WEBSITE: _____

USERNAME: _____

PASSWORD: _____

QUESTION: _____

ANSWER: _____

NOTES: _____

_____

WEBSITE: _____

USERNAME: _____

PASSWORD: _____

QUESTION: _____

ANSWER: _____

NOTES: _____

_____

WEBSITE: _____

USERNAME: _____

PASSWORD: _____

QUESTION: _____

ANSWER: _____

NOTES: _____

_____

C

WEBSITE:

USERNAME:

PASSWORD:

QUESTION:

ANSWER:

NOTES:

WEBSITE:

USERNAME:

PASSWORD:

QUESTION:

ANSWER:

NOTES:

WEBSITE:

USERNAME:

PASSWORD:

QUESTION:

ANSWER:

NOTES:

WEBSITE: _____

USERNAME: _____

PASSWORD: _____

QUESTION: _____

ANSWER: _____

NOTES: _____

_____

WEBSITE: _____

USERNAME: _____

PASSWORD: _____

QUESTION: _____

ANSWER: _____

NOTES: _____

_____

WEBSITE: _____

USERNAME: _____

PASSWORD: _____

QUESTION: _____

ANSWER: _____

NOTES: _____

_____

C

WEBSITE:

USERNAME:

PASSWORD:

QUESTION:

ANSWER:

NOTES:

WEBSITE:

USERNAME:

PASSWORD:

QUESTION:

ANSWER:

NOTES:

WEBSITE:

USERNAME:

PASSWORD:

QUESTION:

ANSWER:

NOTES:

WEBSITE: _____

USERNAME: _____

PASSWORD: _____

QUESTION: _____

ANSWER: _____

NOTES: _____

_____

WEBSITE: _____

USERNAME: _____

PASSWORD: _____

QUESTION: _____

ANSWER: _____

NOTES: _____

_____

WEBSITE: _____

USERNAME: _____

PASSWORD: _____

QUESTION: _____

ANSWER: _____

NOTES: _____

_____

D

WEBSITE:

USERNAME:

PASSWORD:

QUESTION:

ANSWER:

NOTES:

WEBSITE:

USERNAME:

PASSWORD:

QUESTION:

ANSWER:

NOTES:

WEBSITE:

USERNAME:

PASSWORD:

QUESTION:

ANSWER:

NOTES:

D

WEBSITE: _____

USERNAME: _____

PASSWORD: _____

QUESTION: _____

ANSWER: _____

NOTES: _____

_____

WEBSITE: _____

USERNAME: _____

PASSWORD: _____

QUESTION: _____

ANSWER: _____

NOTES: _____

_____

WEBSITE: _____

USERNAME: _____

PASSWORD: _____

QUESTION: _____

ANSWER: _____

NOTES: _____

_____

E

WEBSITE:

USERNAME:

PASSWORD:

QUESTION:

ANSWER:

NOTES:

WEBSITE:

USERNAME:

PASSWORD:

QUESTION:

ANSWER:

NOTES:

WEBSITE:

USERNAME:

PASSWORD:

QUESTION:

ANSWER:

NOTES:

WEBSITE: _____

USERNAME: _____

PASSWORD: _____

QUESTION: _____

ANSWER: _____

NOTES: _____

_____

WEBSITE: _____

USERNAME: _____

PASSWORD: _____

QUESTION: _____

ANSWER: _____

NOTES: _____

_____

WEBSITE: _____

USERNAME: _____

PASSWORD: _____

QUESTION: _____

ANSWER: _____

NOTES: _____

_____

E

WEBSITE:

USERNAME:

PASSWORD:

QUESTION:

ANSWER:

NOTES:

WEBSITE:

USERNAME:

PASSWORD:

QUESTION:

ANSWER:

NOTES:

WEBSITE:

USERNAME:

PASSWORD:

QUESTION:

ANSWER:

NOTES:

WEBSITE:

USERNAME:

PASSWORD:

QUESTION:

ANSWER:

NOTES:

WEBSITE:

USERNAME:

PASSWORD:

QUESTION:

ANSWER:

NOTES:

WEBSITE:

USERNAME:

PASSWORD:

QUESTION:

ANSWER:

NOTES:

F

WEBSITE:

USERNAME:

PASSWORD:

QUESTION:

ANSWER:

NOTES:

WEBSITE:

USERNAME:

PASSWORD:

QUESTION:

ANSWER:

NOTES:

WEBSITE:

USERNAME:

PASSWORD:

QUESTION:

ANSWER:

NOTES:

WEBSITE:

USERNAME:

PASSWORD:

QUESTION:

ANSWER:

NOTES:

WEBSITE:

USERNAME:

PASSWORD:

QUESTION:

ANSWER:

NOTES:

WEBSITE:

USERNAME:

PASSWORD:

QUESTION:

ANSWER:

NOTES:

G

WEBSITE:

USERNAME:

PASSWORD:

QUESTION:

ANSWER:

NOTES:

WEBSITE:

USERNAME:

PASSWORD:

QUESTION:

ANSWER:

NOTES:

WEBSITE:

USERNAME:

PASSWORD:

QUESTION:

ANSWER:

NOTES:

G

WEBSITE: _____

USERNAME: _____

PASSWORD: _____

QUESTION: _____

ANSWER: _____

NOTES: _____

_____

WEBSITE: _____

USERNAME: _____

PASSWORD: _____

QUESTION: _____

ANSWER: _____

NOTES: _____

_____

WEBSITE: _____

USERNAME: _____

PASSWORD: _____

QUESTION: _____

ANSWER: _____

NOTES: _____

_____

G

WEBSITE: _____

USERNAME: _____

PASSWORD: _____

QUESTION: _____

ANSWER: _____

NOTES: _____

_____

WEBSITE: _____

USERNAME: _____

PASSWORD: _____

QUESTION: _____

ANSWER: _____

NOTES: _____

_____

WEBSITE: _____

USERNAME: _____

PASSWORD: _____

QUESTION: _____

ANSWER: _____

NOTES: _____

_____

WEBSITE: _____

USERNAME: _____

PASSWORD: _____

QUESTION: _____

ANSWER: _____

NOTES: _____

_____

WEBSITE: _____

USERNAME: _____

PASSWORD: _____

QUESTION: _____

ANSWER: _____

NOTES: _____

_____

WEBSITE: _____

USERNAME: _____

PASSWORD: _____

QUESTION: _____

ANSWER: _____

NOTES: _____

_____

H

WEBSITE:

USERNAME:

PASSWORD:

QUESTION:

ANSWER:

NOTES:

WEBSITE:

USERNAME:

PASSWORD:

QUESTION:

ANSWER:

NOTES:

WEBSITE:

USERNAME:

PASSWORD:

QUESTION:

ANSWER:

NOTES:

WEBSITE: _____

USERNAME: _____

PASSWORD: _____

QUESTION: _____

ANSWER: _____

NOTES: _____

_____

WEBSITE: _____

USERNAME: _____

PASSWORD: _____

QUESTION: _____

ANSWER: _____

NOTES: _____

_____

WEBSITE: _____

USERNAME: _____

PASSWORD: _____

QUESTION: _____

ANSWER: _____

NOTES: _____

_____

WEBSITE:

USERNAME:

PASSWORD:

QUESTION:

ANSWER:

NOTES:

WEBSITE:

USERNAME:

PASSWORD:

QUESTION:

ANSWER:

NOTES:

WEBSITE:

USERNAME:

PASSWORD:

QUESTION:

ANSWER:

NOTES:

WEBSITE:

USERNAME:

PASSWORD:

QUESTION:

ANSWER:

NOTES:

WEBSITE:

USERNAME:

PASSWORD:

QUESTION:

ANSWER:

NOTES:

WEBSITE:

USERNAME:

PASSWORD:

QUESTION:

ANSWER:

NOTES:

WEBSITE:

USERNAME:

PASSWORD:

QUESTION:

ANSWER:

NOTES:

WEBSITE:

USERNAME:

PASSWORD:

QUESTION:

ANSWER:

NOTES:

WEBSITE:

USERNAME:

PASSWORD:

QUESTION:

ANSWER:

NOTES:

J

WEBSITE:

USERNAME:

PASSWORD:

QUESTION:

ANSWER:

NOTES:

WEBSITE:

USERNAME:

PASSWORD:

QUESTION:

ANSWER:

NOTES:

WEBSITE:

USERNAME:

PASSWORD:

QUESTION:

ANSWER:

NOTES:

WEBSITE:

USERNAME:

PASSWORD:

QUESTION:

ANSWER:

NOTES:

WEBSITE:

USERNAME:

PASSWORD:

QUESTION:

ANSWER:

NOTES:

WEBSITE:

USERNAME:

PASSWORD:

QUESTION:

ANSWER:

NOTES:

J

WEBSITE:

USERNAME:

PASSWORD:

QUESTION:

ANSWER:

NOTES:

WEBSITE:

USERNAME:

PASSWORD:

QUESTION:

ANSWER:

NOTES:

WEBSITE:

USERNAME:

PASSWORD:

QUESTION:

ANSWER:

NOTES:

K

WEBSITE:

USERNAME:

PASSWORD:

QUESTION:

ANSWER:

NOTES:

WEBSITE:

USERNAME:

PASSWORD:

QUESTION:

ANSWER:

NOTES:

WEBSITE:

USERNAME:

PASSWORD:

QUESTION:

ANSWER:

NOTES:

WEBSITE:

USERNAME:

PASSWORD:

QUESTION:

ANSWER:

NOTES:

WEBSITE:

USERNAME:

PASSWORD:

QUESTION:

ANSWER:

NOTES:

WEBSITE:

USERNAME:

PASSWORD:

QUESTION:

ANSWER:

NOTES:

K

WEBSITE:

USERNAME:

PASSWORD:

QUESTION:

ANSWER:

NOTES:

WEBSITE:

USERNAME:

PASSWORD:

QUESTION:

ANSWER:

NOTES:

WEBSITE:

USERNAME:

PASSWORD:

QUESTION:

ANSWER:

NOTES:

WEBSITE: _____

USERNAME: _____

PASSWORD: _____

QUESTION: _____

ANSWER: _____

NOTES: _____

_____

WEBSITE: _____

USERNAME: _____

PASSWORD: _____

QUESTION: _____

ANSWER: _____

NOTES: _____

_____

WEBSITE: _____

USERNAME: _____

PASSWORD: _____

QUESTION: _____

ANSWER: _____

NOTES: _____

_____

L

WEBSITE:

USERNAME:

PASSWORD:

QUESTION:

ANSWER:

NOTES:

WEBSITE:

USERNAME:

PASSWORD:

QUESTION:

ANSWER:

NOTES:

WEBSITE:

USERNAME:

PASSWORD:

QUESTION:

ANSWER:

NOTES:

WEBSITE: _____

USERNAME: _____

PASSWORD: _____

QUESTION: _____

ANSWER: _____

NOTES: _____

_____

WEBSITE: _____

USERNAME: _____

PASSWORD: _____

QUESTION: _____

ANSWER: _____

NOTES: _____

_____

WEBSITE: _____

USERNAME: _____

PASSWORD: _____

QUESTION: _____

ANSWER: _____

NOTES: _____

_____

M

WEBSITE:

USERNAME:

PASSWORD:

QUESTION:

ANSWER:

NOTES:

WEBSITE:

USERNAME:

PASSWORD:

QUESTION:

ANSWER:

NOTES:

WEBSITE:

USERNAME:

PASSWORD:

QUESTION:

ANSWER:

NOTES:

WEBSITE:

USERNAME:

PASSWORD:

QUESTION:

ANSWER:

NOTES:

WEBSITE:

USERNAME:

PASSWORD:

QUESTION:

ANSWER:

NOTES:

WEBSITE:

USERNAME:

PASSWORD:

QUESTION:

ANSWER:

NOTES:

M

WEBSITE: _____

USERNAME: _____

PASSWORD: _____

QUESTION: _____

ANSWER: _____

NOTES: _____

_____

WEBSITE: _____

USERNAME: _____

PASSWORD: _____

QUESTION: _____

ANSWER: _____

NOTES: _____

_____

WEBSITE: _____

USERNAME: _____

PASSWORD: _____

QUESTION: _____

ANSWER: _____

NOTES: _____

_____

WEBSITE:

USERNAME:

PASSWORD:

QUESTION:

ANSWER:

NOTES:

WEBSITE:

USERNAME:

PASSWORD:

QUESTION:

ANSWER:

NOTES:

WEBSITE:

USERNAME:

PASSWORD:

QUESTION:

ANSWER:

NOTES:

N

WEBSITE:

USERNAME:

PASSWORD:

QUESTION:

ANSWER:

NOTES:

WEBSITE:

USERNAME:

PASSWORD:

QUESTION:

ANSWER:

NOTES:

WEBSITE:

USERNAME:

PASSWORD:

QUESTION:

ANSWER:

NOTES:

WEBSITE:

USERNAME:

PASSWORD:

QUESTION:

ANSWER:

NOTES:

WEBSITE:

USERNAME:

PASSWORD:

QUESTION:

ANSWER:

NOTES:

WEBSITE:

USERNAME:

PASSWORD:

QUESTION:

ANSWER:

NOTES:

WEBSITE:

USERNAME:

PASSWORD:

QUESTION:

ANSWER:

NOTES:

WEBSITE:

USERNAME:

PASSWORD:

QUESTION:

ANSWER:

NOTES:

WEBSITE:

USERNAME:

PASSWORD:

QUESTION:

ANSWER:

NOTES:

WEBSITE: _____

USERNAME: _____

PASSWORD: _____

QUESTION: _____

ANSWER: _____

NOTES: _____

_____

WEBSITE: _____

USERNAME: _____

PASSWORD: _____

QUESTION: _____

ANSWER: _____

NOTES: _____

_____

WEBSITE: _____

USERNAME: _____

PASSWORD: _____

QUESTION: _____

ANSWER: _____

NOTES: _____

_____

WEBSITE:

USERNAME:

PASSWORD:

QUESTION:

ANSWER:

NOTES:

WEBSITE:

USERNAME:

PASSWORD:

QUESTION:

ANSWER:

NOTES:

WEBSITE:

USERNAME:

PASSWORD:

QUESTION:

ANSWER:

NOTES:

WEBSITE: _____

USERNAME: _____

PASSWORD: _____

QUESTION: _____

ANSWER: _____

NOTES: _____

_____

WEBSITE: _____

USERNAME: _____

PASSWORD: _____

QUESTION: _____

ANSWER: _____

NOTES: _____

_____

WEBSITE: _____

USERNAME: _____

PASSWORD: _____

QUESTION: _____

ANSWER: _____

NOTES: _____

_____

P

WEBSITE: _____

USERNAME: _____

PASSWORD: _____

QUESTION: _____

ANSWER: _____

NOTES: _____

_____

WEBSITE: _____

USERNAME: _____

PASSWORD: _____

QUESTION: _____

ANSWER: _____

NOTES: _____

_____

WEBSITE: _____

USERNAME: _____

PASSWORD: _____

QUESTION: _____

ANSWER: _____

NOTES: _____

_____

P

WEBSITE:

USERNAME:

PASSWORD:

QUESTION:

ANSWER:

NOTES:

WEBSITE:

USERNAME:

PASSWORD:

QUESTION:

ANSWER:

NOTES:

WEBSITE:

USERNAME:

PASSWORD:

QUESTION:

ANSWER:

NOTES:

WEBSITE:

USERNAME:

PASSWORD:

QUESTION:

ANSWER:

NOTES:

WEBSITE:

USERNAME:

PASSWORD:

QUESTION:

ANSWER:

NOTES:

WEBSITE:

USERNAME:

PASSWORD:

QUESTION:

ANSWER:

NOTES:

WEBSITE: _____

USERNAME: _____

PASSWORD: _____

QUESTION: _____

ANSWER: _____

NOTES: _____

_____

WEBSITE: _____

USERNAME: _____

PASSWORD: _____

QUESTION: _____

ANSWER: _____

NOTES: _____

_____

WEBSITE: _____

USERNAME: _____

PASSWORD: _____

QUESTION: _____

ANSWER: _____

NOTES: _____

_____

WEBSITE: _____

USERNAME: _____

PASSWORD: _____

QUESTION: _____

ANSWER: _____

NOTES: _____

_____

WEBSITE: _____

USERNAME: _____

PASSWORD: _____

QUESTION: _____

ANSWER: _____

NOTES: _____

_____

WEBSITE: _____

USERNAME: _____

PASSWORD: _____

QUESTION: _____

ANSWER: _____

NOTES: _____

_____

WEBSITE: _____

USERNAME: _____

PASSWORD: _____

QUESTION: _____

ANSWER: _____

NOTES: _____

_____

WEBSITE: _____

USERNAME: _____

PASSWORD: _____

QUESTION: _____

ANSWER: _____

NOTES: _____

_____

WEBSITE: _____

USERNAME: _____

PASSWORD: _____

QUESTION: _____

ANSWER: _____

NOTES: _____

_____

R

WEBSITE:

USERNAME:

PASSWORD:

QUESTION:

ANSWER:

NOTES:

WEBSITE:

USERNAME:

PASSWORD:

QUESTION:

ANSWER:

NOTES:

WEBSITE:

USERNAME:

PASSWORD:

QUESTION:

ANSWER:

NOTES:

WEBSITE: _____

USERNAME: _____

PASSWORD: _____

QUESTION: _____

ANSWER: _____

NOTES: _____

_____

WEBSITE: _____

USERNAME: _____

PASSWORD: _____

QUESTION: _____

ANSWER: _____

NOTES: _____

_____

WEBSITE: _____

USERNAME: _____

PASSWORD: _____

QUESTION: _____

ANSWER: _____

NOTES: _____

_____

S

WEBSITE:

USERNAME:

PASSWORD:

QUESTION:

ANSWER:

NOTES:

WEBSITE:

USERNAME:

PASSWORD:

QUESTION:

ANSWER:

NOTES:

WEBSITE:

USERNAME:

PASSWORD:

QUESTION:

ANSWER:

NOTES:

WEBSITE: _____

USERNAME: _____

PASSWORD: _____

QUESTION: _____

ANSWER: _____

NOTES: _____

_____

WEBSITE: _____

USERNAME: _____

PASSWORD: _____

QUESTION: _____

ANSWER: _____

NOTES: _____

_____

WEBSITE: _____

USERNAME: _____

PASSWORD: _____

QUESTION: _____

ANSWER: _____

NOTES: _____

_____

S

WEBSITE:

USERNAME:

PASSWORD:

QUESTION:

ANSWER:

NOTES:

WEBSITE:

USERNAME:

PASSWORD:

QUESTION:

ANSWER:

NOTES:

WEBSITE:

USERNAME:

PASSWORD:

QUESTION:

ANSWER:

NOTES:

WEBSITE: _____

USERNAME: _____

PASSWORD: _____

QUESTION: _____

ANSWER: _____

NOTES: _____

_____

WEBSITE: _____

USERNAME: _____

PASSWORD: _____

QUESTION: _____

ANSWER: _____

NOTES: _____

_____

WEBSITE: _____

USERNAME: _____

PASSWORD: _____

QUESTION: _____

ANSWER: _____

NOTES: _____

_____

T

WEBSITE:

USERNAME:

PASSWORD:

QUESTION:

ANSWER:

NOTES:

WEBSITE:

USERNAME:

PASSWORD:

QUESTION:

ANSWER:

NOTES:

WEBSITE:

USERNAME:

PASSWORD:

QUESTION:

ANSWER:

NOTES:

T

WEBSITE: _____

USERNAME: _____

PASSWORD: _____

QUESTION: _____

ANSWER: _____

NOTES: _____

_____

WEBSITE: _____

USERNAME: _____

PASSWORD: _____

QUESTION: _____

ANSWER: _____

NOTES: _____

_____

WEBSITE: _____

USERNAME: _____

PASSWORD: _____

QUESTION: _____

ANSWER: _____

NOTES: _____

_____

U

WEBSITE:

USERNAME:

PASSWORD:

QUESTION:

ANSWER:

NOTES:

WEBSITE:

USERNAME:

PASSWORD:

QUESTION:

ANSWER:

NOTES:

WEBSITE:

USERNAME:

PASSWORD:

QUESTION:

ANSWER:

NOTES:

U

WEBSITE:

USERNAME:

PASSWORD:

QUESTION:

ANSWER:

NOTES:

WEBSITE:

USERNAME:

PASSWORD:

QUESTION:

ANSWER:

NOTES:

WEBSITE:

USERNAME:

PASSWORD:

QUESTION:

ANSWER:

NOTES:

U

WEBSITE: _____

USERNAME: _____

PASSWORD: _____

QUESTION: _____

ANSWER: _____

NOTES: _____

_____

WEBSITE: _____

USERNAME: _____

PASSWORD: _____

QUESTION: _____

ANSWER: _____

NOTES: _____

_____

WEBSITE: _____

USERNAME: _____

PASSWORD: _____

QUESTION: _____

ANSWER: _____

NOTES: _____

_____

WEBSITE: _____

USERNAME: _____

PASSWORD: _____

QUESTION: _____

ANSWER: _____

NOTES: _____

_____

WEBSITE: _____

USERNAME: _____

PASSWORD: _____

QUESTION: _____

ANSWER: _____

NOTES: _____

_____

WEBSITE: _____

USERNAME: _____

PASSWORD: _____

QUESTION: _____

ANSWER: _____

NOTES: _____

_____

V

WEBSITE:

USERNAME:

PASSWORD:

QUESTION:

ANSWER:

NOTES:

WEBSITE:

USERNAME:

PASSWORD:

QUESTION:

ANSWER:

NOTES:

WEBSITE:

USERNAME:

PASSWORD:

QUESTION:

ANSWER:

NOTES:

WEBSITE: _____

USERNAME: _____

PASSWORD: _____

QUESTION: _____

ANSWER: _____

NOTES: _____

_____

WEBSITE: _____

USERNAME: _____

PASSWORD: _____

QUESTION: _____

ANSWER: _____

NOTES: _____

_____

WEBSITE: _____

USERNAME: _____

PASSWORD: _____

QUESTION: _____

ANSWER: _____

NOTES: _____

_____

WEBSITE:

USERNAME:

PASSWORD:

QUESTION:

ANSWER:

NOTES:

WEBSITE:

USERNAME:

PASSWORD:

QUESTION:

ANSWER:

NOTES:

WEBSITE:

USERNAME:

PASSWORD:

QUESTION:

ANSWER:

NOTES:

WEBSITE:

USERNAME:

PASSWORD:

QUESTION:

ANSWER:

NOTES:

WEBSITE:

USERNAME:

PASSWORD:

QUESTION:

ANSWER:

NOTES:

WEBSITE:

USERNAME:

PASSWORD:

QUESTION:

ANSWER:

NOTES:

WEBSITE:

USERNAME:

PASSWORD:

QUESTION:

ANSWER:

NOTES:

WEBSITE:

USERNAME:

PASSWORD:

QUESTION:

ANSWER:

NOTES:

WEBSITE:

USERNAME:

PASSWORD:

QUESTION:

ANSWER:

NOTES:

WEBSITE:

USERNAME:

PASSWORD:

QUESTION:

ANSWER:

NOTES:

WEBSITE:

USERNAME:

PASSWORD:

QUESTION:

ANSWER:

NOTES:

WEBSITE:

USERNAME:

PASSWORD:

QUESTION:

ANSWER:

NOTES:

X

WEBSITE:

USERNAME:

PASSWORD:

QUESTION:

ANSWER:

NOTES:

WEBSITE:

USERNAME:

PASSWORD:

QUESTION:

ANSWER:

NOTES:

WEBSITE:

USERNAME:

PASSWORD:

QUESTION:

ANSWER:

NOTES:

WEBSITE:

USERNAME:

PASSWORD:

QUESTION:

ANSWER:

NOTES:

WEBSITE:

USERNAME:

PASSWORD:

QUESTION:

ANSWER:

NOTES:

WEBSITE:

USERNAME:

PASSWORD:

QUESTION:

ANSWER:

NOTES:

Y

WEBSITE:

USERNAME:

PASSWORD:

QUESTION:

ANSWER:

NOTES:

WEBSITE:

USERNAME:

PASSWORD:

QUESTION:

ANSWER:

NOTES:

WEBSITE:

USERNAME:

PASSWORD:

QUESTION:

ANSWER:

NOTES:

Y

WEBSITE:

USERNAME:

PASSWORD:

QUESTION:

ANSWER:

NOTES:

WEBSITE:

USERNAME:

PASSWORD:

QUESTION:

ANSWER:

NOTES:

WEBSITE:

USERNAME:

PASSWORD:

QUESTION:

ANSWER:

NOTES:

Y

WEBSITE:

USERNAME:

PASSWORD:

QUESTION:

ANSWER:

NOTES:

WEBSITE:

USERNAME:

PASSWORD:

QUESTION:

ANSWER:

NOTES:

WEBSITE:

USERNAME:

PASSWORD:

QUESTION:

ANSWER:

NOTES:

Z

WEBSITE: _____

USERNAME: _____

PASSWORD: _____

QUESTION: _____

ANSWER: _____

NOTES: _____

_____

WEBSITE: _____

USERNAME: _____

PASSWORD: _____

QUESTION: _____

ANSWER: _____

NOTES: _____

_____

WEBSITE: _____

USERNAME: _____

PASSWORD: _____

QUESTION: _____

ANSWER: _____

NOTES: _____

_____

Z

WEBSITE:

USERNAME:

PASSWORD:

QUESTION:

ANSWER:

NOTES:

WEBSITE:

USERNAME:

PASSWORD:

QUESTION:

ANSWER:

NOTES:

WEBSITE:

USERNAME:

PASSWORD:

QUESTION:

ANSWER:

NOTES:

Z

WEBSITE: _____

USERNAME: _____

PASSWORD: _____

QUESTION: _____

ANSWER: _____

NOTES: _____

_____

WEBSITE: _____

USERNAME: _____

PASSWORD: _____

QUESTION: _____

ANSWER: _____

NOTES: _____

_____

WEBSITE: _____

USERNAME: _____

PASSWORD: _____

QUESTION: _____

ANSWER: _____

NOTES: _____

_____

NOTES:

NOTES:

NOTES:

NOTES:

NOTES:

NOTES:

NOTES:

NOTES:

NOTES:

NOTES:

NOTES:

NOTES:

NOTES:

NOTES:

NOTES: